T0197446

I Am Made of Coal!

Leigh Ann Ray

Archway Publishing books may be ordered through booksellers or by contacting:

Archway Publishing
1663 Liberty Drive
Bloomington, IN 47403
www.archwaypublishing.com
1 (888) 242-5904

ISBN: 978-1-4808-3818-5 (sc)
ISBN: 978-1-4808-3821-5 (e)

Print information available on the last page.

Archway Publishing rev. date: 10/6/2016

Acknowledgements

Special thanks to Williamson Fire Department Chief Joey Carey and local photographer Sonya Hatfield Hall for allowing use of photos from the Coal House fire.

I am the Coal House. I am made of coal.

Coal is a mineral that looks like a black rock.

Coal is very important because it provides the energy needed
to produce electricity used around the world every day.

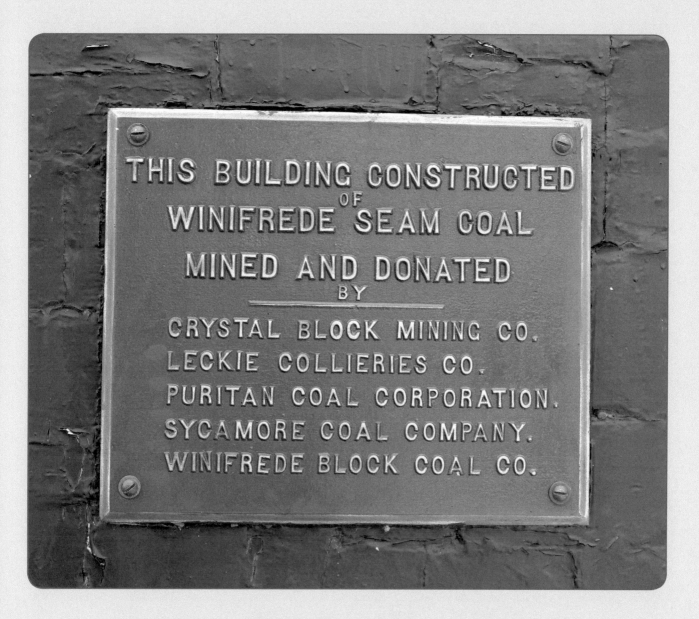

THIS BUILDING CONSTRUCTED
OF
WINIFREDE SEAM COAL
MINED AND DONATED
BY

CRYSTAL BLOCK MINING CO.
LECKIE COLLIERIES CO.
PURITAN COAL CORPORATION.
SYCAMORE COAL COMPANY.
WINIFREDE BLOCK COAL CO.

I was built in 1933 from 65 tons of coal mined from the
Winifrede seam in Mingo County, West Virginia.

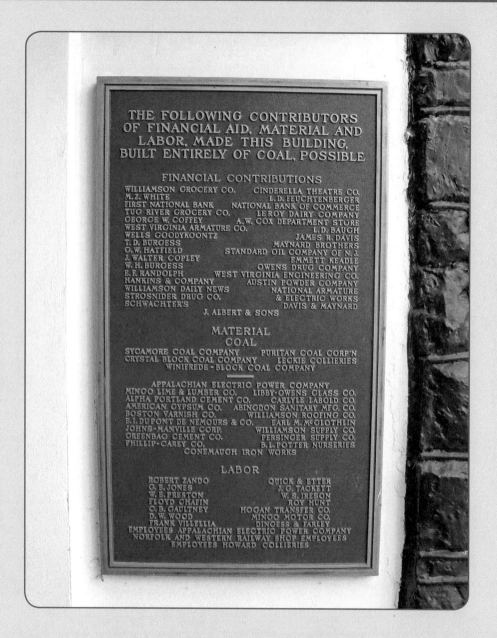

THE FOLLOWING CONTRIBUTORS
OF FINANCIAL AID, MATERIAL AND
LABOR, MADE THIS BUILDING,
BUILT ENTIRELY OF COAL, POSSIBLE

FINANCIAL CONTRIBUTIONS

WILLIAMSON GROCERY CO.	CINDERELLA THEATRE CO.
M. Z. WHITE	L. D. FEUCHTENBERGER
FIRST NATIONAL BANK	NATIONAL BANK OF COMMERCE
TUG RIVER GROCERY CO.	LE ROY DAIRY COMPANY
GEORGE W. COFFEY	A. W. COX DEPARTMENT STORE
WEST VIRGINIA ARMATURE CO.	
WELLS GOODYKOONTZ	L. D. BAUGH
T. D. BURGESS	JAMES R. DAVIS
G. W. HATFIELD	MAYNARD BROTHERS
J. WALTER COPLEY	STANDARD OIL COMPANY OF N. J.
W. H. BURGESS	EMMETT KEADLE
B. F. RANDOLPH	OWENS DRUG COMPANY
HANKINS & COMPANY	WEST VIRGINIA ENGINEERING CO.
WILLIAMSON DAILY NEWS	AUSTIN POWDER COMPANY
STROSNIDER DRUG CO.	NATIONAL ARMATURE
SCHWACHTER'S	& ELECTRIC WORKS
	DAVIS & MAYNARD

J. ALBERT & SONS

MATERIAL
COAL

SYCAMORE COAL COMPANY	PURITAN COAL CORP'N
CRYSTAL BLOCK COAL COMPANY	LECKIE COLLIERIES

WINIFREDE - BLOCK COAL COMPANY

APPALACHIAN ELECTRIC POWER COMPANY

MINGO LIME & LUMBER CO.	LIBBY-OWENS GLASS CO.
ALPHA PORTLAND CEMENT CO.	CARLYLE LABOLD CO.
AMERICAN GYPSUM CO.	ABINGDON SANITARY MFG. CO.
BOSTON VARNISH CO.	WILLIAMSON ROOFING CO.
E. I. DUPONT DE NEMOURS & CO.	EARL M. McGLOTHLIN
JOHNS-MANVILLE CORP.	WILLIAMSON SUPPLY CO.
GREENBAG CEMENT CO.	PERSINGER SUPPLY CO.
PHILLIP-CAREY CO.	B. L. POTTER NURSERIES

CONEMAUGH IRON WORKS

LABOR

ROBERT ZANDO	QUICK & ETTER
O. E. JONES	J. C. TACKETT
W. B. PRESTON	W. S. IRESON
FLOYD CHAFIN	ROY HUNT
O. B. GAULTNEY	HOGAN TRANSFER CO.
D. W. WOOD	MINGO MOTOR CO.
FRANK VILLELLIA	DINGESS & FARLEY

EMPLOYEES APPALACHIAN ELECTRIC POWER COMPANY
NORFOLK AND WESTERN RAILWAY SHOP EMPLOYEES
EMPLOYEES HOWARD COLLIERIES

I was built as a symbol for the "Billion Dollar Coal Field", the heart of which lies in Williamson, West Virginia, where I stand.

When I was built, I was the only building made of coal. Now, I am one of only two buildings built from this mineral.

When I was built, I was only intended to be a monument to the coal industry and its importance to the Tug Valley area.

But, to everyone's surprise, I became a key part of our community. I am very important to Williamson.

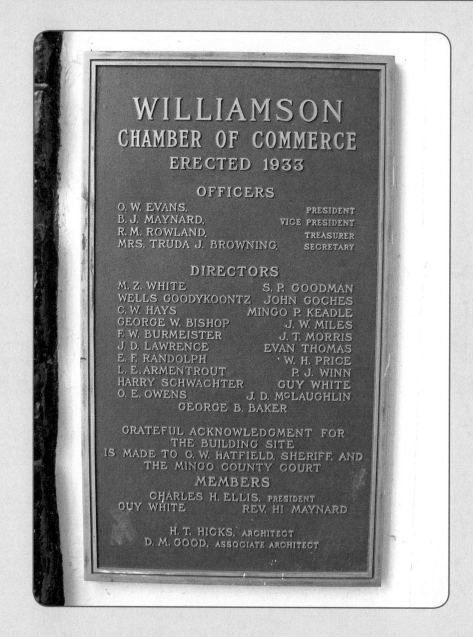

WILLIAMSON
CHAMBER OF COMMERCE
ERECTED 1933

OFFICERS

O. W. EVANS,   PRESIDENT
B. J. MAYNARD,   VICE PRESIDENT
R. M. ROWLAND,   TREASURER
MRS. TRUDA J. BROWNING,   SECRETARY

DIRECTORS

M. Z. WHITE   S. P. GOODMAN
WELLS GOODYKOONTZ   JOHN GOCHES
C. W. HAYS   MINGO P. KEADLE
GEORGE W. BISHOP   J. W. MILES
F. W. BURMEISTER   J. T. MORRIS
J. D. LAWRENCE   EVAN THOMAS
E. F. RANDOLPH   W. H. PRICE
L. E. ARMENTROUT   P. J. WINN
HARRY SCHWACHTER   GUY WHITE
O. E. OWENS   J. D. McLAUGHLIN
           GEORGE B. BAKER

GRATEFUL ACKNOWLEDGMENT FOR
THE BUILDING SITE
IS MADE TO G. W. HATFIELD, SHERIFF, AND
THE MINGO COUNTY COURT
MEMBERS
CHARLES H. ELLIS, PRESIDENT
GUY WHITE   REV. HI MAYNARD.

H. T. HICKS, ARCHITECT
D. M. GOOD, ASSOCIATE ARCHITECT

I am home to the Tug Valley Chamber of Commerce and
the Williamson Convention and Visitor's Bureau.

People from all over the world come to see me every year. When people visit me, they learn about the coal industry, the Hatfield-McCoy Feud, and many other exciting things that have taken place in the Tug Valley.

THE COAL HOUSE
BUILT · 1933
NATIONAL REGISTER OF HISTORIC PLACES

I am so unique that in March 1980, I was added to the National Park Service's Register of Historic Places. This is a list of buildings that are different or rare and considered to be special.

On Columbus Day in 2010, a great tragedy occurred.

A fire started inside my ceiling. Flames shot through my roof and out my windows, damaging everything.

Thankfully, the Williamson Fire Department came
to my rescue and put the fire out quickly.

I suffered a lot of damage. Smoke and water ruined EVERYTHING. Furniture, books, photographs – it all had to be thrown into the trash.

My owners, the Mingo County Commission,
didn't know if I could be saved.

Despite the fact that I had suffered so much damage, people still came to see me. They didn't care that I was boarded up and they couldn't come inside. They still wanted to see me, still wanted to take pictures of me.

Though I was glad people were still interested in me, I was very sad because they couldn't come inside or see what I had been like before the fire.

One day, some very nice people came to see me. They brought tools and supplies. They replaced chunks of coal that had been damaged during the removal of things ruined by the fire.

They lifted off what was left of my old roof and replaced it with a new one; they gave me new windows and a new entryway.

They built and painted new walls and hung new lights. They even gave me a new floor.

They worked very hard and when they were
done, I was brand new again!

I am now even stronger than when I was first built. The news that
I had been saved was so exciting that even the governor of West
Virginia came to see me and a young couple had their wedding here.

Today, I continue to welcome visitors from all over the
world to the Tug Valley. I like it when people come
to see me and learn about our area's history.

I am very proud to be made of coal.

Printed in the United States
by Baker & Taylor Publisher Services